Baby Moose on the Loose

Baby Moosey Moosey Gets Lost in Anchorage

C. J. Halsey

Illustrated by Christa Scheck

Copyright © 2017 Carole Jean Halsey
Illustrated by Christa Scheck
All rights reserved.
Island City Publishing LLC
Okemos, Michigan
www.islandcitypublishing.com
ISBN-13: 978-1-946890-04-7
Library of Congress Control Number 2017953228
Printed in the USA

DEDICATION

This book is dedicated to my granddaughters; Sharon Gaile, who was 3 years old and Leora Lynn, who was 2 years old; residing in Gallup, New Mexico at the time of the creation of this story. They encouraged the telling of the story with their giggles and saying "Tell it again, Grandma!" while visiting me and traveling back and forth the five miles between my home and their aunt's home. I love them and miss them when they are not around.

In Alaska, the land of the Midnight sun, where the summers are short, and the winters are long, there are the most beautiful sun rises and sun sets. The rivers are wide and winding. The fish are huge. The mountains are tall, and the moose run wild.

In the Municipality of Anchorage, Alaska there lived two brothers, Evan and Austen.

One morning the boys decided to get up early for school to surprise their Mom. They washed, dressed and ate before their mom's alarm went off.

Austen looked out the window and shouted to Evan, "Hurry! There's a Baby Moosey Moosey in our front yard."

Evan looked out, amazed at the baby moose asleep in their yard.

They carefully opened the door and peeked their heads out. Baby Moosey Moosey lifted his head to look at the brothers.

"Why are you sleeping in our front Yard? Where is your mother?" Evan asked Baby Moosey Moosey.

Baby Moosey Moosey began to cry. "I lost my Mama Moosey Moosey! I looked everywhere. I got so tired, I laid down here and I went to sleep."

"We'll help you find your Mama Moosey Moosey," Austen told Baby Moosey Moosey. "Wait here. We need to get our coats on."

The brothers went inside, wrote a note to their mom, put on their coats, hats, scarves, mittens and boots. They grabbed a scarf for Baby Moosey Moosey.

The boys looked all around the outside of their house.

No Mama Moosey Moosey! Poor Baby Moosey Moosey!

They looked all around and under the cars in the street. They went in all the neighbors' yards, front and back.
　No Mama Moosey Moosey! Poor Baby Moosey Moosey!

They walked down the street looking for Mama Moosey Moosey. They came to a gas station. They looked all around it. No Mama Moosey Moosey! Poor Baby Moosey Moosey!

They walked on until they came to a grocery store. They walked all around the outside of it. They went inside. They walked up the aisles. They walked down the aisles.

No Mama Moosey Moosey! Poor Baby Moosey Moosey!

They walked and came to a museum. They walked around it.

They went inside and looked at all the pretty pictures. They looked at all the beautiful sculptures. They even looked at a whale exhibit.

No Mama Moosey Moosey! Poor Baby Moosey Moosey!

They walked to Evan and Austen's school. They looked all around. They looked around the playground. They even looked under the monkey bars.

No Mama Moosey Moosey! Poor Baby Moosey Moosey!

They went to the teacher parking lot and looked under the cars.

"Maybe we should look inside," suggested Austen.

They went inside and looked in all the classrooms. The children were surprised to see a moose at school.

No Mama Moosey Moosey! Poor Baby Moosey Moosey!

"I have a terrific idea," said Evan. "Let's go see Mr. Adams. He'll know what to do."

They made their way to the principal's office.

"Mr. Adams, Baby Moosey Moosey can't find his Mama Moosey Moosey. Can you help us?" asked Austen.

"I know just the right person to call," said Mr. Adams. He picked up the phone and called Mr. Lee, the State Park Ranger.

Ranger Lee came right over. "I would be happy to help find Mama Moosey Moosey," said Ranger Lee. "I saw a Mama Moosey Moosey on the Seward Highway earlier this morning."

"Can we go with you?" asked Austen. "Sure," said Ranger Lee. They all climbed into Ranger Lee's truck and they headed up the road. They went south on Seward Highway

Ranger Lee took the O'Malley exit and headed up Hillside Road towards Flat Top Mountain in the Chugach Mountain Range. "I just know we can find Mama Moosey Moosey somewhere around Flat Top," said Ranger Lee.

The road curved up the foothill and down the foothill. They went around a corner and then up another hill. They went through the spruce trees.

No Mama Moosey Moosey! Poor Baby Moosey Moosey!

They stopped in a parking lot at the base of Flat Top Mountain and got out. Evan and Austen could not believe their eyes.

"Look, we can see all of Anchorage, Wasilla, the Knik Arm, and Cook Inlet. It is so beautiful!" the brothers exclaimed.

The sun rose in pretty shades of pink, purple, blue, and orange.

"Look!" pointed Ranger Lee. "You can see Mount Denali, as the natives call it, meaning 'The High One.'"

The boys were excited and shouted, "It's all covered with snow!" As excited as they were, they were all still sad.

No Mama Moosey Moosey! Poor Baby Moosey Moosey!

"We may have to hike around Flat Top," said Ranger Lee. "There is a lake, Williwaw Lake, that has a stream that flows out of it. I believe we will find Mama Moosey Moosey there."

They all hiked around the mountain.

At Williwaw Lake, Baby Moosey Moosey began to cry. He could not see his Mama Moosey Moosey.

"Don't cry Baby Moosey Moosey, we will keep looking," said Austen.

No Mama Moosey Moosey! Poor Baby Moosey Moosey!

They came to the lake and started walking around it. They came to a very large boulder and looked behind it. Behind the boulder was the start of the stream. They walked downstream and around another curve, and what did they see?

Standing in the middle of the stream was...
Mama Moosey Moosey!

She looked up and was glad to see Baby Moosey Moosey. She went right up to him and started licking him on the nose.

"Thank you for finding Baby Moosey Moosey and bringing him to me," Mama Moosey Moosey said.

"How did you lose him?" asked Evan.

"We went to Anchorage to look for food and got separated crossing the Seward Highway," said Mama Moosey Moosey.

"I looked everywhere for him. I was afraid I would never see him again. Thank you so very much."

They all left the stream. Ranger Lee dumped some of the animal feed he had in his truck on the ground so Mama Moosey Moosey and Baby Moosey Moosey would have food to eat.

Happy Mama Moosey Moosey! Happy Baby Moosey Moosey!

Ranger Lee and the brothers said goodbye. Evan and Austen continued to wave goodbye to Baby Moosey Moosey and called out as Ranger Lee drove away, "We will miss you! Come visit us again!"

Alaska Facts

Alaska is the largest state in the United States of America.

The state capital is Juneau.

Alaska has also been nicknamed "Last Frontier," and "Great Land."

The highest North American peak is in Alaska. It was formally known as Mount McKinley, and was officially renamed to Denali in 2015.

The state bird is the Willow Ptarmigan.

The state flower is the Forget-Me-Not.

The state colors are blue and gold.

The state tree is the Sitka Spruce.

The state mineral is Gold.

The state sport is Dog Mushing.

The state fish is the Giant King Salmon.

The state land mammal is the

MOOSE.

ABOUT THE AUTHOR

CJ Halsey was born and raised in Michigan but lived ten years in Alaska. In Alaska, it was common to find a moose in your yard. While in Alaska she fell in love with the beauty of the land and wanted to share that love with others.

She and her husband Karl now live in Michigan. Together they have five children, 18 grandchildren, and six great grandchildren.

Her goal in writing this story is to encourage children and their parents to always show love to one another; also to inspire a desire to travel the great state of Alaska.

NOTES FROM THE AUTHOR

I would like to thank my children Leora, John, and Stephanie for encouraging me to put my stories on paper, and my husband's cousin, Robert for the encouragement to get the story published. I am thankful for Dee Cassidy who edited my book and gave great encouragement and Celeste Bennett of Island City Publishing LLC for publishing this book.

Parents: If you have the pleasure of visiting Anchorage, and love to hike and camp, Flattop Mountain and the Williwaw Lake Trails are in the Chugach Mountains just a short 20 minute drive northeast of Anchorage, Alaska.

Camping and hiking enthusiasts can find out more about camping and hiking near Flattop at http://alaska.org or http://dnr.alaska.gov/.

A NOTE FROM THE PUBLISHER

If you enjoyed this book by CJ Halsey, please let others know about it and consider leaving a review on Amazon.com. Thank you!

Made in the USA
Las Vegas, NV
22 February 2021